THE STORY OF KAMALA HARRIS

A Biography Book for New Readers

—— Written by ——
Tonya Leslie, PhD

—— Illustrated by ——
Juanita Londoño

ROCKRIDGE
PRESS

To all the brave girls who break down
barriers and stand up for justice.

Series Designer: Angela Navarra
Interior and Cover Designer: Angela Navarra
Art Producer: Sue Bischofberger

Editor: Mary Colgan
Production Editor: Jenna Dutton
Production Manager: Jose Olivera

Illustration © 2021 Juanita Londoño; maps courtesy of Creative Market.
Photography © Renee Brouchard/Library of Congress, p. 47;
Scott Morris/Alamy Stock Photo, p. 49; Stefani Reynolds/Bloomberg via Getty Images, p. 50;
author photo courtesy of Christina Morassi; illustrator photo courtesy of Santiago Alzate.

ISBN: Print 978-1-64876-537-7 | eBook 978-1-64876-538-4
R0

CONTENTS

CHAPTER 1

A LEADER IS BORN

Meet Kamala Harris

Kamala Harris has always been for the people. As a lawyer, an **attorney general**, a US **senator**, and now the vice president of the United States, her whole life has been dedicated to working for **justice**.

While she was fighting for others, Kamala also broke down several **barriers** for many different groups of people. She is the first Black American and South Asian American vice president. She's also the first woman vice president, but she won't be the last! In everything she's done, Kamala has worked to make sure that other people also have equal access to opportunity and justice.

Kamala always knew that the world was bigger than her. As a young child, she traveled to her parents' home countries—Jamaica and India. She even lived in Canada! Throughout her travels, Kamala was always interested in the ways that people were fighting for fairness. She knew that she wanted to do something to help. That drive led her to be a lawyer, a senator, and ultimately the vice president.

Her story is still unfolding. What will she do next?

 **Kamala's World**

Kamala Devi Harris was born in Oakland, California, on October 20, 1964. Her parents were both **immigrants**. They came to the United States from other countries so that they could study at college. Kamala's father, Donald

Harris, came from Jamaica to study **economics**, and her mother, Shyamala Gopalan, came from India to study science.

In the 1960s, the world was changing. College students all over the country were taking part in the fight for **civil rights**. Black and white college students were riding buses together into the segregated South and sitting at lunch counters in peaceful protest. These actions helped end the laws of **segregation**, which kept Black and white people separated.

My mother had a saying:
Kamala, you may be the first
to do many things, but make
sure you're not the last.

Donald and Shyamala met on their college
campus while they were fighting for justice.
They got married in 1963. That was the same
year Martin Luther King Jr. made his famous
"I Have a Dream" speech. A year later, Kamala
was born.

Kamala (pronounced *COMMA-la*) means
"lotus flower" in Sanskrit. Sanskrit is an
ancient language of India and is believed
to be the oldest language in the world. The
lotus flower is an important symbol in Indian
culture. The beautiful flower appears to float
on water, even though it is rooted firmly in the
mud below.

Kamala became interested in civil rights and the fight for justice early on. She often attended protest marches with her parents. She would watch the sea of **protestors** from

her stroller. Along with her parents, she would follow the protestors and raise her fist. Power to the people!

WHEN?

Kamala's parents meet at college.	Kamala's parents marry.	Kamala is born.
1962	**1963**	**1964**

CHAPTER 2

THE EARLY YEARS

 Growing Up

Kamala's early years in California were happy and carefree. Her sister, Maya, was born in 1967, and their house was filled with music and food. Education was also very important to the Harris family. Both of Kamala's parents spent a lot of time studying, and books were everywhere. Kamala's dad taught classes, and her mother worked at a lab. She was looking for a cure for cancer. The family liked to take trips together, too. Kamala got to see her dad's family in Jamaica, and she visited her mother's family in India.

Kamala learned that fighting for justice ran in her family. Her grandfather fought for the freedom of Indian people. For many years, India was ruled by Britain, but the Indian people wanted to be free. In 1947, India gained independence. Kamala's grandfather would tell her stories about the fight for freedom while

they walked on the beach. He told her how important it was to fight for **democracy**.

When Kamala was seven, her father got a job at the University of Wisconsin. He was going to move away to teach. This was hard on the marriage, and eventually Kamala's parents divorced. Kamala remembered that the only thing her parents argued about when they divorced was who got all the books.

Kamala and Maya would see their father on weekends and in the summer. During the rest of the time, they lived with their mother.

They went with her to protests, and their house was always filled with interesting people who talked about making the world a better place.

✧ Finding Her Way ✧

Kamala was always a warrior for justice. Before she was born, schools had been segregated. Black and white children did not go to school together. But the civil rights movement changed the laws. One way to bring different children together was to bus them all to the same school. So, every day when Kamala went to school, she got onto a big yellow bus that took her out of her neighborhood and across town. This was called **integration**.

Kamala didn't really know that word at the time. All she knew was that her school was made up of different friends who spoke different languages. She loved it. So, when her mother decided to move to Canada to take a new job, Kamala and Maya were disappointed. The city of Montreal was far away. And it was cold! They would be leaving the warm weather of California for a snowy winter wonderland. Also, people in Montreal spoke French. Could a lotus flower survive the cold?

The Harris Family

BERYL
CHRISTIE

OSCAR
JOSEPH
HARRIS
(1914–1976)

RAJAM
GOPALAN

P. V.
GOPALAN
(1911–1998)

DONALD
J. HARRIS
(1938–
PRESENT)

SHYAMALA
GOPALAN
(1938–2009)

KAMALA
HARRIS
(1964–
PRESENT)

MAYA
HARRIS
(1967–
PRESENT)

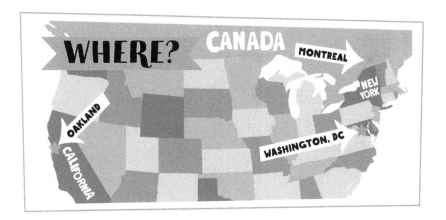

Kamala did! She even staged her first protest in Montreal. Kamala learned that children weren't allowed to play on the lawn in front of her apartment building. It didn't seem fair. Kamala and Maya marched in protest. Eventually, the building manager changed the rules. The children were free to play on the lawn. Kamala's first protest was a success!

JUMP -IN THE- THINK TANK

Kamala lived in different places and experienced different cultures. How might this have shaped how she saw the world?

Kamala liked life in Canada, but she missed America. That's why when she graduated from high school, she decided to return to the United States to go to college. She enrolled at Howard University in Washington, DC.

WHEN?

Kamala's sister, Maya, is born.	Kamala's parents get divorced.	Kamala moves to Montreal in Canada.	Kamala attends Howard University.
1967	**1972**	About **1977**	**1982**

CHAPTER 3

KAMALA THE LAWYER

A New Career

Howard University is a historically Black school in Washington, DC. Many famous civil rights leaders went there, including Thurgood Marshall, a Supreme Court justice. It seemed like the perfect place for Kamala. She made a lot of friends. And she also worked hard. Kamala studied how the government worked and continued to lead protests. One summer, she interned with a senator and learned what it meant to work in a public office and fight for justice. After she graduated, Kamala went back to California to study law. She attended the University of California, Hastings College of the Law, in Berkeley. There she decided to become a **prosecutor**.

A prosecutor is a lawyer who proves that someone is guilty. Kamala chose to be this kind of lawyer because she saw a lot of injustice around her. As a prosecutor, she could make sure that people who committed crimes were held responsible.

After law school, Kamala took the bar exam. That's the test that allows a person to practice law. Kamala didn't pass! She was devastated, but she didn't give up. Instead, she studied harder and took the test again. The second time, she passed. Finally, Kamala could follow her dreams.

Can you think of a time when you didn't give up on your dream? What kept you going?

Kamala's first job was as the deputy district attorney in Alameda, a city next to Oakland where she was raised. Later, she worked in different offices in California, gaining experience helping people. Then she took a job in an office that worked on behalf of families and children. There, Kamala could not only help individual families, but she could also work on the policies, or laws and rules, that could help families all over the state.

 ## **Life in San Francisco**

In San Francisco, Kamala led the child services division of city hall. In that role, she brought charges against people who committed crimes that hurt children. Kamala worked to get families into safe spaces and keep them away from harm. It was important work, and Kamala knew that it really mattered.

Protecting innocent people was just one part of her job. Another part of her job was helping change policies and laws so that people always had access to safety and fairness. Kamala began to make recommendations for more funding, so she could help even more families.

Kamala knew that she wanted to do more. So, she decided to run for the office of district attorney.

Anyone who claims to be a leader must speak like a leader. That means speaking with integrity and truth.

A **district attorney** (DA) is the lead prosecutor of a county. The DA manages other lawyers and is the person who decides what cases to prosecute. The lawyers the DA manages are not elected to office, but the DA is. To be the district attorney of San Francisco, Kamala would have to run a political **campaign** to get votes.

WHEN?

Kamala graduates from Howard.	Kamala passes the bar exam.	Kamala becomes a deputy district attorney.
1986	**1990**	**1990**

CHAPTER 4

WORKING FOR JUSTICE

Running for Office

Kamala didn't have a lot of money or experience running a campaign. But she knew that in order to be elected as district attorney, she had to go out and meet people in the **community**. Before they could support her, people had to know who she was and what she stood for. Kamala's mother helped her get the word out. Together, they set up an ironing board in front of the local supermarket and other public areas. The ironing board made the perfect standing desk! They taped up posters and spoke to people about Kamala's plans. Kamala would meet and greet people who went in and out of the store.

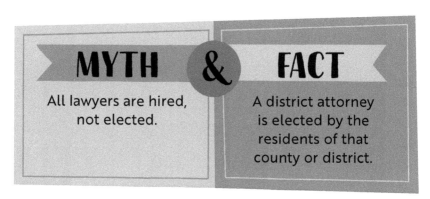

MYTH & FACT

All lawyers are hired, not elected.

A district attorney is elected by the residents of that county or district.

She asked questions so she could find out what was important to the community. People asked her questions, too. They wanted to know more about her life.

Other people were running for the office, too. The first round of the election ended in a tie. Kamala made the top two candidates. Then there was a second election. She won! Kamala celebrated the win with her family. She was now the first woman to become the DA of San Francisco.

Her first days on the job weren't easy. The office was a mess! One of the first things Kamala did was paint the walls. She always believed no problem was too small to fix. Now the office was ready for the important work that needed to be done.

An Important Job

Kamala got to work. She met families who suffered because of gang violence. She pushed for laws that made sure guilty people went to jail and stayed there. But Kamala knew that some people who were charged with crimes didn't need to be punished. Instead, they needed help. Kamala understood that one bad choice can lead a good person to a challenging situation. She looked for ways to stop the cycles that kept people from getting ahead. Not everyone agreed with her approach.

Kamala decided that the community needed programs to help people who had made mistakes

get their lives back on track. In fact, she called her program Back on Track. Then Kamala met a woman named Lateefah Simon. Lateefah made bad decisions as a young woman, but she was able to get help and change her life. Then she began to make different choices. She even won an award for a program she started to help girls in tough situations. Kamala asked Lateefah to help with Back on Track, and Lateefah agreed. Now Lateefah and Kamala were helping women all around the city get a fresh start.

JUMP —IN THE— THINK TANK

Have you ever made a bad choice? What happened? What did you learn?

Kamala continued to set her sights high. She decided to run for the California attorney general office. An attorney general is the head lawyer of a state or even a country. Kamala began another campaign to win votes. But this time, her mother couldn't help. Shyamala was sick. Then, in 2009, her mother died from cancer. Kamala knew that she had to honor her mother's memory by working hard to help others. So, that's what she continued to do.

WHEN?

Kamala is elected as DA of San Francisco.	Kamala's mother dies.	Kamala becomes California attorney general.
2003	**2009**	**2010**

CHAPTER 5

BREAKING
BARRIERS

$\mathcal{L}\mathcal{L}$ A New Role $\mathcal{L}\mathcal{L}$

On January 3, 2011, Kamala became the first woman in California history to be elected to the attorney general's office. She was also the first Black woman to hold that position, as well as the first South Asian woman. That's a lot of firsts! But Kamala didn't focus on that. Instead, she focused on doing good work.

As the attorney general, Kamala was the top lawyer in the whole state. Her job was to make sure that every voice in California mattered. People in California were having a hard time. Some people were losing their homes because they had bad loans. Several years earlier, the banks began to make risky loans to people, loans that the people wouldn't be able to pay back. The people needed help. Kamala started investigating. She wanted to hold the banks responsible. California is a big state with a lot of economic power. Kamala used this power to

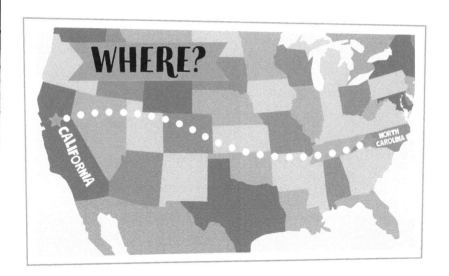

negotiate with the country's five biggest banks. She made sure the banks would help people keep their homes.

In 2012, Kamala announced an agreement with the biggest technology companies to be more open about how they used people's private information. She also worked to help prison inmates. Instead of just throwing people in jail, Kamala fought to get them education and job training. And she had other **priorities,** like protecting the environment. Kamala won huge settlements against the oil companies that caused oil spills. Kamala became well-known throughout all of California.

Then, in 2012, Kamala was asked to speak at the Democratic National **Convention** in North Carolina. At a convention, a political party chooses who will be the candidate for the presidential election. In 2012, the Democrats were standing behind Barack Obama. He was running for a second term as president.

When Kamala took the stage, people across the country saw a rising star. People began to learn about her good work and wanted to know more about her.

Moving Up

Kamala had a lot going on and was working all the time. Her friends thought she needed to have some fun. So they introduced her to a lawyer named Doug Emhoff. Kamala and Doug got along, but Kamala was worried. Doug had two children, named Cole and Ella. Would they like her? They did! In 2014, Kamala and Doug got married. They wanted to make sure that their wedding included traditions from both of their cultures. Doug stomped on a glass as part of his Jewish culture. Kamala put flowers around his neck as part of her Indian culture.

Why do you think cultural traditions are important to Kamala? Does your family have any?

The children even got involved. They
came up with the perfect name for their
new stepmom—Momala!

Balancing life and work was challenging.
Kamala began a new family tradition of having
Sunday dinner at home together. She had more
responsibility at work now, so she had to work
hard to keep her family traditions alive.

What I want young
women and girls to know is:
You are powerful and
your voice matters.

Kamala thought about how she could do more for her community. As a lawyer, she brought people to justice. But she wondered how she could help change laws and stop injustices before they happened. Then in 2015, Barbara Boxer, one of California's senators, announced that she wouldn't be running for reelection. Kamala thought about it. As a senator, she would be able to do even more for her state. She would be able to help change laws. It would be more work, but it would be worth it.

Many people believed Kamala would be a good senator, and they spoke up for her. First, the state's governor, Jerry Brown, endorsed her. Then President Obama and Vice President

Joe Biden gave her the thumbs-up. In November 2016, the election came and Californians cast their votes. Kamala won! In her victory speech, Kamala talked about fighting for the rights and equality of all people. She thought about her mother and the work she had done. Kamala felt she was walking in her footsteps. She was using her voice to help others.

WHEN?

Kamala becomes attorney general.	Kamala speaks at the Democratic Convention.	Kamala marries Doug Emhoff.
2011	**2012**	**2014**

CHAPTER 6

HARRIS
★ ★ ★
SENATOR-ELECT

SENATOR

HARRIS

Working in Washington

Though senators represent their states, they spend most of their time in Washington, DC, working with others in the government. That's where they pass new laws. Now that she was a senator, Kamala didn't see her family as often. Still, she tried to make it home for Sunday dinner. She wanted to stay connected to her family and to the community she worked for.

In Washington, Kamala worked on a lot of the same issues she fought for in California. Only now she was able to create laws that would help people. She continued to work for families.

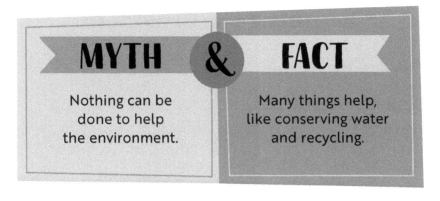

She helped pass laws that would help immigrant children find safe places to live. And she worked hard to protect the environment. Every year, wildfires burn homes in California. Scientists say changes to the environment will make the fires worse. Kamala worked to help people understand these issues, so laws could be passed that would make things better.

Kamala was working hard and making important changes to the laws. Still, she thought, *What more could I do?* Then she decided there was one more thing. She could run for president.

On January 21, 2019, Kamala announced on TV that she was running to become the president of the United States. The day was significant because it was Martin Luther King Jr. Day. She used the slogan "For the People." The first time Kamala set foot in a courtroom, she stood up and proudly said to the judge, "Kamala Harris, for the people." Kamala always stood up to protect the rights of the people. People knew that she was on their side.

Kamala's presidential campaign was much harder than her earlier ones in California. She needed more than an ironing board desk! She needed offices. Naturally, she chose Oakland, California, for one of her campaign offices. The other thing she needed was money, so she could afford to get her message out. Kamala traveled all around the country. She spoke at different events and went on TV. She told people about her work and what she would do if she became president.

Then it was time for the presidential debates. That's when all the candidates running for office get together to talk about and compare their plans. The debates help people decide who to vote for. Kamala did well in the debates and defended her position. But on December 3, 2019, she decided to end her campaign.

JUMP —IN THE— THINK TANK

Have you ever had to end something to try something new?

Many other candidates were also in the race, and it was hard for Kamala to stand out. When she stepped aside, it marked the end of one journey and the start of something else. Another candidate, former vice president Joe Biden, went on to win the nomination. He would be the Democratic candidate for president. But Joe saw something special in Kamala. So, he asked Kamala to join him. If he won, she would be the vice president!

WHEN?

Kamala becomes a US senator.	Kamala runs for president.	Joe Biden announces Kamala as his running mate.
2016	**2019**	**2020**

CHAPTER 7

BECOMING VICE PRESIDENT

Many Firsts

On August 19, 2020, Kamala prepared to take the stage. Once again, she was going to speak at the Democratic National Convention. But things were different this time. Now she was the candidate for vice president. Also, most of the seats would be empty. A deadly **virus** called COVID-19 had spread across the country and the world. People were getting sick. In order to stay healthy, people wore masks and stayed apart. The convention would take place in Wisconsin, but people had to watch it at home on TV to make sure everyone stayed safe.

Kamala was used to campaigning, but not like this. Before, she would shake hands and give hugs as she went around meeting new people. Now she had to stay apart. When Election Day came in November, many people didn't want to go out to vote in person. They didn't want to risk getting sick. Instead, they mailed in their ballots.

Usually, a winner is announced on Election Night or early the next day, after all the votes are counted. Because so many people voted by mail, some people worried that not all votes would be counted. The officials knew they wouldn't be able to count all the votes in one night. They knew it might take several days. And they couldn't rush. They didn't want to make any mistakes. Finally, after four long days, it was official. Joe Biden and Kamala Harris would be the new president and vice president of the United States!

Kamala wore a white suit when she made her acceptance speech on Saturday, November 7, 2020. Her white suit was a symbol of all the women before her who had fought for the right to vote. Remembering those women, Kamala said, "I stand on their shoulders."

**JUMP
–IN THE–
THINK
TANK**

COVID-19 changed how people voted. Has it changed anything in your life? How?

Kamala Harris makes history as the first woman vice president of the United States. She is also the first Jamaican American and the first Indian American to hold that office. Kamala talked about all of these firsts in her speech. "While I may be the first woman in this office," Kamala said, "I will not be the last, because every little girl watching tonight sees that this is a country of possibilities."

MYTH & FACT

MYTH: Everyone has always had the right to vote in the United States.

FACT: Women only began to get the right to vote in 1920, which was 100 years before the first woman became vice president.

Kamala's Legacy

On January 20, 2021, Kamala was sworn in as vice president. Standing in front of the Capitol Building in Washington, DC, with Doug at her side, she held up her right hand and swore to support and defend the **Constitution of the United States**. Joe Biden made the same promise. A few hours later, Kamala gave her first speech as vice president. With the Washington Monument behind her, she spoke of American **aspiration**, calling Americans bold, fearless, and ambitious. These are the same traits that Kamala's mother inspired in her.

Kamala had reached the next stage in a journey she began as a little girl in a stroller, attending protests with her parents.

As a child, Kamala watched her parents fight for justice. Then she followed in their footsteps. Throughout her career, she kept pushing to make sure that people had the help they needed. As a lawyer, she fought to protect people's rights.

And to the children of our country, regardless of your gender, our country has sent you a clear message: Dream with ambition, lead with conviction, and see yourself in a way that others might not see you, simply because they've never seen it before. And we will applaud you every step of the way.

As a senator, she fought to create laws that would protect people. What will she do next? Her legacy as vice president is still being written.

WHEN?

Kamala runs for president.	Kamala is chosen to run for vice president.	Kamala becomes vice president.
2019	**2020**	**2021**

CHAPTER 8

SO...WHO IS

KAMALA HARRIS ?

Challenge Accepted!

Now that you have met Vice President Kamala Harris, let's test your new knowledge in a little who, what, when, where, why, and how "quiz." Feel free to look back in the text to find the answers if you need to, but try to remember first!

1 **When was Kamala born?**

→ A 1920
→ B 1964
→ C 2019
→ D 2021

2 **Which two countries were Kamala's parents from?**

→ A India and Jamaica
→ B India and Canada
→ C Jamaica and California
→ D Washington, DC, and California

3   What does Kamala's name mean?

→ A   Leader

→ B   Rose

→ C   Lotus flower

→ D   Lawyer

4   What college did Kamala attend?

→ A   New York University

→ B   California State University

→ C   The University of Toronto

→ D   Howard University

5   What was Kamala NOT the first to be?

→ A   First woman to vote

→ B   First woman to be attorney general in California

→ C   First woman to become vice president

→ D   First Indian American to become vice president

6 Who is Kamala's sister?

→ A Shyamala

→ B Lateefah

→ C Diana

→ D Maya

7 What did Kamala and her mother use as a table for her first campaign?

→ A A card table

→ B A moving box

→ C A desk

→ D An ironing board

8 **What do Kamala's stepchildren call her?**

→ A Stepmom

→ B Momala

→ C Mom

→ D Kamala

9 **Who chose Kamala to be vice president?**

→ A Barbara Boxer

→ B Barack Obama

→ C Joe Biden

→ D Martin Luther King Jr.

10 **In what way has Kamala changed the world?**

→ A She has been the first woman to hold many major positions.

→ B She started the civil rights movement.

→ C She is a lawyer.

→ D She has gone to college.

Our World

Kamala has always stood for justice. She likes to say that she is for the people. Here are some other ways Kamala changed the world.

→ Kamala started Back on Track, a program that helps people who have been in prison go on to have successful lives.

→ Kamala has worked on a program called Open Justice, so that people can see what was going on in their communities.

→ In 2019, Kamala wrote a children's book called *Superheroes Are Everywhere*, inspiring children to look for superheroes in everyday life and be the best they can be.

JUMP
—IN THE—
THINK
TANK
FOR

MORE!

Kamala's passion for justice inspired her to be a lawyer. But she soon realized she could help people in many ways. That led her to take on more and more leadership roles.

→ Kamala is passionate about fighting for justice. What are some of your passions? Do you have one main passion or many things you are passionate about?

→ People help each other every day, in ways either big or small. How do you think kids can help people in their family, school, or community? Can you think of something small you can do to make someone's day better?

→ Kamala wrote a children's book to encourage kids to be their best selves. Why do you think she wanted to do this? Has a book ever inspired you to try something new?

Glossary

ambition: A goal or aim

aspiration: A strong hope or desire to achieve something

attorney general: The head lawyer of a state or a country

barrier: Something that blocks the way or makes things difficult

campaign: The activities that help a person reach a goal

civil rights: Basic rights that every person has under the laws of the government including to be treated fairly and equally

community: A group of people living or working together

Constitution of the United States: A document written in 1787 right after the United States first became a country, which states the basic laws, instructions, and rules for how the country must be run

convention: A large meeting that brings together groups of people to discuss shared issues

conviction: A strong belief

district attorney: The lead prosecutor of a county, also called a DA

democracy: A form of government in which people have a say in how the government is run

economics: The science of money, goods, and services

immigrant: A person born in one country who moves to another country and settles there

integration: The end of a policy that keeps people apart, usually based on their race or skin color

justice: Fairness

priority: Something more important than other things

prosecutor: A lawyer who tries to prove someone is guilty of a crime

protestors: People who organize to express their disapproval of something

segregation: The separation of people, usually based on their race or skin color

senator: A member of the Senate whose job it is to represent their state in the federal government

virus: A type of germ that creates disease

Bibliography

Books

Harris, Kamala. *The Truths We Hold: An American Journey*. New York: Penguin Books, 2020.

Harris, Kamala, and Ruby Shamir. *The Truths We Hold: An American Journey*. Young Readers Edition. New York: Penguin Books, 2020.

Schwartz, Heather E. *Kamala Harris: Madam Vice President*. Minneapolis: Lerner Publications, 2021.

Articles

Bilefsky, Dan. "In Canada, Kamala Harris, a Disco-Dancing Teenager, Yearned for Home." *New York Times*. October 5, 2020, NYTimes .com/2020/10/05/world/canada/kamala-harris-montreal.html.

Herndon, Astead W. "What Kamala Harris Learned about Power at Howard." *New York Times*. October 14, 2020. NYTimes.com/2020/10/14 /us/politics/kamala-harris-howard.html.

Igoe, Katherine J., and Bianca Rodriguez. "Who Is Kamala Harris's Dad Donald Harris, a Renowned Stanford Professor?" *Marie Claire*. Last modified January 19, 2021. MarieClaire.com/politics/a28259825 /who-is-donald-harris-kamala-harris-father.

Miller, Korin. "Who Are Kamala Harris' Parents? 16 Things to Know about the Vice President's Family." *Women's Health*. Last modified January 20, 2021. WomensHealthMag.com/life/a33581601/kamala-harris-parents.

About the Author

TONYA LESLIE, PhD, is a writer and a researcher. She lives between New York and Belize. As a Black woman, she was thrilled when Kamala Harris became vice president! When she's not writing and researching, Tonya enjoys going to the beach.

About the Illustrator

JUANITA LONDOÑO is a children's book, editorial, and commercial illustrator from Medellín, Colombia. She has a degree in animation concept art from the Vancouver Film School. Juanita has worked for clients like Simon & Schuster, HarperCollins, Target, American Greetings, and Quarto. She likes drawing characters and environments with vibrant colors, textured details, and emotions to bring people on a journey. Juanita relishes seeing life through the lens of magical realism that is so deeply connected to her Latin American roots.

WHO WILL INSPIRE YOU NEXT?

EXPLORE A WORLD OF HEROES AND ROLE MODELS IN
THE STORY OF... BIOGRAPHY SERIES FOR NEW READERS.

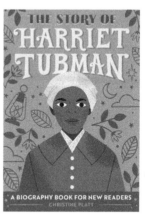

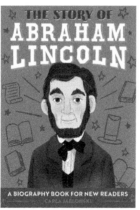

LOOK FOR THIS SERIES
WHEREVER BOOKS AND EBOOKS ARE SOLD

Alexander Hamilton

Albert Einstein

Martin Luther King Jr.

George Washington

Jane Goodall

Barack Obama

Helen Keller

Marie Curie

CPSIA information can be obtained
at www.ICGtesting.com
Printed in the USA
JSHW051953240921
18951JS00002BA/3